YOU MUST REMEMBER THIS

1968

MILESTONES, MEMORIES,
TRIVIA AND FACTS, NEWS EVENTS,
PROMINENT PERSONALITIES &
SPORTS HIGHLIGHTS OF THE YEAR

TO : _____

FROM : _____

MESSAGE : _____

_____

selected and researched
by
mary a. pradt

WARNER ⓦ TREASURES ™

PUBLISHED BY WARNER BOOKS

A TIME WARNER COMPANY

Warner Books, Inc.
1271 Avenue of the Americas
New York, New York 10020

Warner Treasures is a
trademark of Warner Books, Inc.

A Time Warner Company

DESIGN:
CAROL BOKUNIEWICZ DESIGN
PRINTED IN SINGAPORE
FIRST PRINTING : MAY 1995
10 9 8 7 6 5 4 3 2 1
ISBN : 0-446-91045-7

The Vietnam war and the cause of racial and social justice became rallying points in 1968. Social unrest was evident in the form of protests, riots, and other disorders.

1968

Any survey or poll in the U.S. and probably on the planet, that sought to identify the most significant year in the second half of the 20th century, would come up with the same result: 1968. This was the tumultuous year that included: the assassinations of Dr. Martin Luther King and Bobby Kennedy; one of the most memorable presidential elections ever; the full flowering of the Student Revolution worldwide, and the coming-of-age of the "Counterculture," which began to invade the mainstream culture. It's often been said, "If you remember the sixties, you probably weren't really there."

richard m. nixon

Republican candidate, with Spiro Agnew as running mate, won the election by about half a million votes. It was one of the closest elections and most remarkable political comebacks in history.

newsreel

The presidential race was up for grabs. Senators Robert F. Kennedy and Eugene McCarthy both entered the fray as liberal, antiwar candidates. As the country was still reeling from the April assassination of Dr. Martin Luther King, Jr., and the riots that followed, Bobby Kennedy was killed by Sirhan Sirhan, a young Arab, June 6 in L.A., after winning the California primary. A lot of dreams died with King and Kennedy.

The protests culminated in August when the Democratic National Convention was held in Chicago. Thousands of students and protesters gathered outside, camping out in Lincoln Park. Tear gas filled the air as TV cameras rolled, filming the Chicago police beating the demonstrators.

'68

headlines

riots and revolution

After the assassination of Dr. King, blacks rioted in more than 100 cities. Hardest hit were Chicago, Baltimore, Washington, and Cincinnati. Many parts of Washington and other cities were reduced to smoldering piles of rubble. Students, fueled by antiwar and antiracist beliefs, began to assert themselves on college campuses around the country. Most notable was the revolt at Columbia University in New York City, which began April 22, 1968. Mark Rudd, leader of the Columbia chapter of Students for a Democratic Society, led students who held the college dean hostage in his office for 24 hours.

Czechoslovakia experienced a wave of political liberalization that became known as Prague Spring. Later, Russian and Warsaw Pact forces moved in with tanks to crush the budding democratic movement.

Student protests swept Europe. Workers and students nearly paralyzed France with their protests and strikes. Millions of workers seized factories, and DeGaulle was forced to raise the minimum wage by 35 percent.

HAIR, the "tribal love-rock musical," moved to Broadway from its downtown venue. Many performers got their start either in the Broadway production or in one of the many touring companies — Disco queen Donna Summer, pudgy singer Meat Loaf, and actress Diane Keaton, to name a few.

HAIR ★ HAIGHT ★ ACID ★ BLISS ★ PEACE ★ LOVE

haight-ashbury,

A SLIGHTLY SLUMMY SECTION OF SAN FRANCISCO, BECAME DE FACTO CENTER OF THE HIPPIE MOVEMENT. CRASH PADS, "FREE STORES," DAY-GLO PAINT AND PSYCHEDELIC POSTERS WERE AMONG THE HAIGHT'S FEATURES THAT PARENTS AND OTHER ADULTS LOVED TO HATE. DRUGS WERE AROUND; THE ARRAY RANGED FROM A TO Z, WITH LSD A SPECIAL FAVORITE.

THE BEATLES, BORED WITH FAME AND FORTUNE, WENT TO INDIA TO SEEK "ABSOLUTE BLISS CONSCIOUSNESS" WITH MAHARISHI MAHESH YOGI. ON THEIR RETURN, THEY PRODUCED THE FAMOUS **WHITE ALBUM.**

cultural
milestones

The ubiquitous symbol of 1968 would have to be the peace symbol; originally the logo of SANE, an antinuclear coalition, this simple but powerful design appeared on posters, pendants, graffiti, clothing, and almost everywhere else — instant shorthand for everything the emerging counterculture stood for — or against.

laugh-in was innovative — a groundbreaking show that incorporated sketch comedy, quick takes, fade-outs, recurring characters, and coinages like "You bet your bippy" and "Verrrry interesting," which became instant vernacular. The show launched many careers, but perhaps the biggest star to emerge was Goldie Hawn, who started as a go-go dancer on the show. Everyone wanted to make a guest appearance and did, including Billy Graham and Richard Nixon.

In 1968 there were more than 56 million TV households in the U.S., according to A.C. Nielsen figures. The percentage of American homes with TV had reached 94.6. And what were we watching in prime time?

top-rated shows of the 1968 fall season :

1. "Rowan & Martin's Laugh-In" (NBC)

2. "Gomer Pyle, U.S.M.C." (CBS)

3. "Bonanza" (NBC)

4. "Mayberry R.F.D." (CBS)

5. "Family Affair" (CBS)

6. "Gunsmoke" (CBS)

7. "Julia" (NBC)

8. "The Dean Martin Show" (NBC)

9. "Here's Lucy" (CBS)

10. "The Beverly Hillbillies" (CBS)

julia,
a warm, rather saccharine family series starring Diahann Carroll, was the first to star an African-American woman. The year 1968 was, in fact, a watershed year for Black-oriented programming.

D E A T H S

Marcel Duchamp
French painter, considered the spiritual father of Pop Art, died October 1.

Helen Keller author and humanitarian who overcame deafness and blindness to become symbol of indomitable courage, died June 1 at the age of 87.

Charles William Mayo surgeon and director of the Mayo Clinic who also served at the United Nations, died July 28.

Lurleen Wallace governor of Alabama who was elected to continue the administration of her husband, George Wallace, who was legally forbidden to succeed himself, died May 7.

births

ADAM RICH, who played Nicholas Bradford in "Eight Enough" and later earned the title "heartbreak kid" for his multipl failures at rehab for substance-abuse problems, born October 12.

GARY COLEMAN, who also got his start as a child acto and became a troubled adult, born February 8.

TRACI LORDS, born Nora Louise Kuzma in 1968 (exact da elusive), overcame her background as a teen porn queen who posed nuc in **Penthouse** at 15 and descended into drug addiction; cleaned up her ac and played in TV's "Tommyknockers" and several John Waters films.

MOLLY RINGWALD, major actress of the eighties an nineties, born February 18.

CROWN PRINCE FELIPE JUAN PABLC (DE TODOS LOS SANTOS BORBÓN SCHLESWIG-HOLSTEIN BORBÓ SONDERBURG GLUCKSBURG), the only son and future successor t King Juan Carlos I of Spain, born January 20.

milestones

MARY LOU RETTON, gymnast and Olympic medal ist, born January 24.

ADAM GRAVES, New York Rangers' MVP in Hockey i 1993 and NHL All Star in 1994, was also born in 1968.

JOAN BAEZ, CRYSTALLINE-VOICED FOLK SINGER, MARRIED FELLOW PEACE ACTIVIST DAVID HARRIS IN MARCH.

weddings of the year

jacqueline bouvier kennedy, widow of the slain president, married Greek shipping magnate and multimillionaire **aristotle onassis** in October 1968. This was the most discussed union of the year; many irrationally felt betrayed by our national icon's remarriage.

'68

1. **hey jude** the Beatles. Charted in the Top 40 for 19 weeks, this tune was unusual; its playing time was 7 minutes 11 seconds, at a time when most singles ran two to three minutes.

2. **i heard it through the grapevine** Marvin Gaye. This much-covered tune later became the hugely successful slogan of the California Raisin Board.

3. **love is blue** Paul Mauriat

4. **honey** Bobby Goldsboro

5. **people got to be free** The Rascals

6. **(sittin' on) the dock of the bay** Otis Redding

hit music

more musical hits

hello, i love you The Doors

harper valley p.t.a. Jeannie C. Riley

born to be wild Steppenwolf

chain of fools Aretha Franklin

jumpin' jack flash Rolling Stones

the look of love Sergio Mendes & Brasil '66

7. **this guy's in love with you** Herb Alpert

8. **mrs. robinson** Simon and Garfunkel

9. **love child** Diana Ross and the Supremes

10. **tighten up** Archie Bell and the Drells

BOOKENDS/SIMON & GARFUNKEL

fiction

1. **airport**
   arthur hailey

2. **couples**
   john updike

3. **the salzburg
   connection**
   helen macinnes

4. **a small town
   in germany**
   john le carré

5. **testimony
   of two men**
   taylor caldwell

6. **preserve
   and protect**
   allen drury

7. **myra breckenridge**
   gore vidal

8. **vanished**
   fletcher knebel

9. **christy**
   catherine marshall

10. **the tower
    of babel**
    morris i. west

nonfiction

1. **better homes
   and gardens
   new cookbook**

2. **random house
   dictionary of the
   english language,**
   college edition laurence
   urdang, editor in chief

3. **listen to the warm**
   rod mckuen

4. **between parent
   and child**
   haim g. ginott

5. **lonesome cities**
   rod mckuen

6. **the doctor's quick
   weight loss diet**
   erwin m. stillman and
   samm sinclair baker

7. **the money game**
   adam smith

8. **stanyan street
   & other sorrows**
   rod mckuen

9. **the weight watcher's
   cook book**
   jean nidetch

10. **better homes
    and gardens eat
    and stay slim**

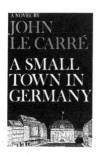

A NOVEL BY
JOHN
LE CARRÉ
A SMALL
TOWN IN
GERMANY

books

FEW NATIONAL OR INTERNATIONAL
EVENTS WERE MIRRORED IN THE YEAR'S
BESTSELLING BOOKS — MORE
WOULD COME IN THE SEVENTIES.

There were a variety of protests before the summer games opened. Black athletes, led by activist and sociologist Harry Edwards, boycotted the New York Athletic Club track meet. The International Olympic Committee voted to readmit South Africa to the games. Black African countries, the Communist bloc, some Asian and Arab countries, and Black Americans threatened to boycott the Olympics. The IOC reversed itself, and South Africa was out of the games.

VINCE LOMBARDI'S GREEN BAY PACKERS BESTED THE OAKLAND RAIDERS IN THE SUPER BOWL.

N A YEAR OF HE PITCHER, OMINATED Y DENNY CCLAIN OF ETROIT AND OB GIBSON F ST. LOUIS, HE TIGERS DGED THE ARDINALS IN HE WORLD ERIES.

In Pasadena, the University of Southern California team beat Indiana 14-3 in the Rose Bowl

sports

Arthur Ashe broke a major color barrier in sports. The young former army officer became the first Black male to win a major tennis tournament when he captured the United States Open championship at Forest Hills in September 1968.

Billie Jean King won her third straight Wimbledon tennis title in July 1968. She was the first woman to win the title three times running since Maureen Connolly achieved the feat in 1952-54. With Rosie Casals, she also won the women's doubles competition.

17

MEMORABLE FILMS

2001: A SPACE ODYSSEY • BARBARELLA
CANDY • CHITTY CHITTY BANG BANG
FUNNY GIRL • I LOVE YOU, ALICE B. TOKLAS
THE ODD COUPLE • YELLOW SUBMARINE
ROMEO AND JULIET • ROSEMARY'S BABY

JANE FONDA
IN *BARBARELLA*

oscars went to

Oliver! as Best Picture; **Cliff Robertson** as Best Actor, for his title role in *Charly*; and **Katharine Hepburn,** Best Actress for the second year in a row, for her role in *The Lion in Winter*. **Jack Albertson** won as Best Supporting Actor for his role in *The Subject Was Roses*. **Ruth Gordon** was Best Supporting Actress for her memorable turn in *Rosemary's Baby*. Directing honors went to **Carol Reed** for *Oliver!*

18

the graduate was the #1 box-office hit of 1968. Starring Dustin Hoffman, and Anne Bancroft as the older woman who seduced him, the film featured Simon & Garfunkel music, most notably "Mrs. Robinson." This movie proved a metaphor for the concerns of confused middle-class youth in 1968.

GUESS WHO'S COMING TO DINNER THE INTERRACIAL ROMANCE BETWEEN SIDNEY POITIER AND KATHARINE HOUGHTON, WITH SPENCER TRACY AND KATHARINE HEPBURN AS THE WHITE WOMAN'S PARENTS, WAS GROUNDBREAKING MOVIE FARE FOR ITS TIME.

movies

'68

Cadillac's front-wheel-drive luxury car, the Eldorado, had debuted in 1967. The 1968 model was a 472-cubic-inch V-8 — the largest displacement of any V-8 at the time. Buick's Wildcat was sportier, with special side trim.

If you wanted to stay in the realm of Ford Motor Company vehicles, you might have liked the Lincoln Continental Mark III in 1968.

wheels

If, however, you were part of the counterculture, your vehicle of choice would have been a VW Bug, possibly painted in psychedelic swirls.

...ught it for its luxury—but all he talks about is performance. Owners of 1968 Cadillacs are so ...stic about the alert response and smooth, quiet operation of the new 472 V-8 engine, that they often fail to mention ... outstanding features. Your authorized Cadillac dealer will be delighted to point out the brilliant new interiors and ... innovations such as concealed windshield wipers and improved variable-ratio power steering. ... wheel and you, too, will experience performance that's remarkably bold and exhilarating! *Cadilla...*

1968 Cadillac Hardtop Sedan deVille

the american luxury car - circa 1968

fashion 1968

FASHION WAS WHATEVER
YOU WANTED IT TO BE:
CAFTANS . LEATHER
VESTS . LONG HAIR
LOVE BEADS . PEACE-
SYMBOL PENDANTS
SANDALS . FACIAL HAIR
FOR MEN . GRANNY

fashion

DRESSES . INDIAN
PRINTS . FLOWER
POWER . PETER MAX
PATTERNS . DAISHIKIS
BLACK BERETS
SHADES, OF COURSE

You could spend more
for the "designer ver-
sion" of any of these
looks. High fashion
was profoundly influ-
enced by street fashion.

23

Three men in a spacecraft, Apollo 8, traveled a half-million miles and became the first men to orbit the Moon. From this distance, they beamed back televised pictures of the far side of the Moon and sent back images of the Earth as seen from the Moon. Their Christmas-night message and the pictures the astronauts sent gave us a different view

final factoid

of our beleaguered planet. From space, one could see no borders, no conflicts, no poverty, no hunger, no apparent suffering. Maybe that's when we began to think it was a planet worth saving.

25